the roots of a thousand embraces

the roots of a thousand embraces

dialogues

juan felipe herrera

manic d press
san francisco

Library of Congress Cataloging-in-Publication Data

Herrera, Juan Felipe.
  The roots of a thousand embraces: dialogues / Juan Felipe Herrera.
    p. cm.

    ISBN 978-1-933149-96-7   (previous edition: ISBN 0-916397-28-9)
    1. Kahlo, Frida--Poetry. 2. Women painters--Mexico--Poetry.
  I. Title
  PS3558.E74R66   1994
  811'.54--dc20   94-29222
                                                       CIP

CONTENTS

In 1993, Manic D Press received a poetry manuscript in the mail with a friendly note. The writer had lived in San Francisco in the late 1980s and was part of the Mission poets scene, a Latino crew that included Jorge Argueta and Francisco X. Alarcon. He was currently teaching in the Chicano/Latin American Studies Department at California State University at Fresno, and was asking that the manuscript be considered for publication.

It was an unusual work: 40 cantos, written as interconnected prose poems, ostensibly about the life of well-known Mexican painter Frida Kahlo. As I read and re-read the work, it became apparent that while it was about Frida Kahlo, it also revealed subtexts open to interpretation, metaphorically and otherwise. Its many messages intrigued me, and I am still in admiration.

Manic D published this manuscript in April 1994—it was the poet's sixth book—in a small edition because Manic D had not yet signed a distribution deal. It received little notice at the time of publication but has stood its ground unwaveringly over the years as a compelling poetic work. Some of the ideas expressed within seem prescient, especially in light of recent political machinations.

As the decades passed, the writer published many books. He has reached the highest acclaim offered to an American poet: after serving as California Poet Laureate, he was appointed the Poet Laureate Consultant in Poetry to the Library of Congress—commonly referred to as the United States Poet Laureate, the nation's official poet.

With the utmost delight and deepest respect, Manic D Press presents readers with a significant early work by Juan Felipe Herrera.

Jennifer Joseph
San Francisco, California

the roots of a thousand embraces

dialogues

Yo soy la desintegración.
— Frida Kahlo
Journals, 1954. Mexico City.

Prologue
A Second Body

Think on the time it takes a scar to heal,

a river to rise — an old woman to regain the tumbling
powers of her busted arms — a young woman (calling
herself Frida) to re-structure her shattered vertebrae, to
be caught up with a body-cast, a second body which she
inhabits — for the rest of her life; this is precious to me,
that is all.

She painted herself somewhere in-between Mexico and
the United States — in the open space of the jaws; between
the mandibles of the jaguar and the nuclear turbine.

It is the healing of this metaphysical fracture too (which
may invoke further breakage) that concerns me.

I
Mobius

Maybe, here, the body

or appreciation is in the degrees of light, non-line and
texture, especially when the light shaft becomes obscure,
half-lit – when it goes into the sutures behind the gesso of
the cast.

There is no top, no bottom – and of course, no beginning
or end, since one body leads into the other – a mobius
body with one side only and a backside we will never
see, logically; there are only beginnings.

I will repeat all this often. There are no time frames,
really.
It goes against the notion of love.

II
Reddish Guitars

A warning:

there is no need to go to extraneous materials for further elaboration – this is a shabby old university ploy; for the moment the Academy is out of reach. Later we may go back to the rat box if we wish. Yours and mine.

There is only one little favor that I ask of you – look up as often as you can, there is something caught up there, loosening – falling, shrapnel-like, shiny; hear it so singly, so able, yet so singly unsure of its residence and celestial dominions.

Now, I pick up my reddish guitar, honey-like, you pick up yours. You pick up yours – is this all we have?

Look up. O, yes, look up.

III
The Ants, the Lizards & the Hawk

I see Frida more often now.

There was a time when I saw her kicking the petty shards among the hopeful and I wouldn't think anything of it. I see her more often now. The shards are sugary and last beyond the expectations of many; they have faces, ivory, and wooden translucent arms. Ants come, always. The lizard gathers heat here.

And the hawk stands on a wire, nearby.

IV
Jade Mother Goddess

Frida came back and kicked away the features.
There was a crisis.

There was a mid-point of no return:
a reddish ovum with tidal waves turning and leaping
beyond its plasma, a jade mother goddess with cactus
shoulders and a puzzled clay-like background broken,
moving around the granite complexion of the moon;
there was a maguey thorn breast, succulent, shedding a
tear-shaped milk drop and in the center, in one of the
centers, there was a scarlet woman with her black hair
falling down into the roots of a thousand embraces. She
reached it alone. And language, (Master-made language)
faltered for a moment, fell apart – yet the Master keeps
on, somehow.

Pretending to speak; writing with the idea that his words
connect with a larger universal system of Master-
meanings. The small invention is simple – this sweaty
speakerly Master.

V
Glyphs, Foliage

Too much energy

and movement by the hand (the Master-hand) has been
forced onto letters on paper.

I have not seen anyone, lately, reaching for the vowels
and crazy consonant glyphs that break through every
foliage, wave, table, throat; a Frida-woman running
across the boulevard, laughing at the small inventions
made by masked men. Who would have thought of it?
The disinherited were busy responding.

We were busy at work – inventing the weapons against
the Master-tongue. Invention was our calling, we
thought – we even prayed, at times for a new chisel, a
fancy scrawl-maker to arrive unannounced at the front
gate. The laughter is well deserved – the Master is feeble
and his enemies (even if in only-fragments) – (we) gather
on occasion, float over the grained glass and break forth
into finer pieces that go against the all-seeing eye.

VI
Frida's Bed

We carry something

different that up to this point has been indecipherable,
(under the most prolonged campaigns of scrutiny by the
Master-scalpel). This is good. It even has been said that
we belong to the clinic.

There is an idea of sickness attached to the figure of our
re-assigned body. Our shatterings have been taken into
high account. (Of course, the Master-surgeon admitted
that it was an accident – maybe, there is a sense of guilt,
remorse, bad training.) A rush order is in the making –
the clinic awaits us.

At home, they point to Frida's bed, an art-bed-studio
where we can rehearse our limbs: the torso that twitches
at midnight. And the left foot, still immobilized in the
sack of a pink squid.

Everything seems to be in our reach now – especially
paint and canvas. We are left with the choice of re-
figuring ourselves – however, mostly in a supine
position, laying down in the bed, staring at the canopy

with a mirror; once in a while we will look out from our
clinic sheets: the syrup colored doorway bends, a
staircase reminds us of prolongation and the varying
degrees of music that lead upwards (the walls are made
of volcanic stone, the kind that has a porous, blackish
skin that breathes and hums like Peruvian quenas with
furious winds at the tips).

A meticulous aura permeates (as in all clinics).

The rain comes down quietly outside, nurturing the
small garden that we can no longer reach with our new
cast bones.

VII
Fuselage Rail

Frozen nihilism,

gesso on the pillow, gesso on the thorax, videos of a
chained figure wearing an exotic shoelace around the
neck – the ivory tipped cigarette holder (of discourse); all
artifacts at the Master's gazebo, his museum.

Shadows:

for us there are no modernisms or post-modernities.
Time is not a savior. It doesn't matter if the
dismemberment takes place in the past. By its very
nature any killing occurring in the past will sweep its
magnetic tides into the future. We have no claim to
Modernism or its aloof, loose-handed twin, Post
Modernism. Only the invasions; *Chaketas* – grayish twill
sheets, body-casts, boundaries on our plot, our words – a
busted fuselage rail jammed through Frida's eighteen-
year-old pubis.

Please see this. This is all there is today, here, at the
floating table.

VIII
Supplications w/Cigarette

The Master-voice

intervenes with supplications: won't you stay a little
longer? Won't you dine with us – for a while, light the
cigarette – enjoy the lampshade of the tent? You are
welcome now and later you will be here, with us, longer.
Stay for a while and speak.

IX
Tropical Parrots

For us

there are no Macro-worlds. No footing where we can re-adjust our language and our shape. No enjambments for our signification. No ready-made molds for our migrant-shard body, breath. We do not wait to build our muscularity, our rebel tendon world. Too many have tried and failed; an old reflex taken from the Master's theatre.

We accept our small numeral, our tiny half-face, our shriveled embryos – this is why what is in vogue does not attract us, this is why what is on sale at the Master's bazaar would be an ill fitting. The Modern-word died at the hands of the few silver tie surgeons; rugged and refined ventriloquists of conquest.

Here, in the tundra – there is chalkdust, tropical parrots – a screaming metro ambulance, maybe, a city with a woman in the shape of a thorn by a lake that waited for an eagle to descend long ago.

X
The Master Stage

We claim no territory.

No language for further disclosures of who and what we are. There is no need for us to seek audition at the Master's stage.

We say – *we do not live here.*

Nor do we inhabit the market palace; there are too many translators in the aisles. It is enough that Frida lives. This is good.

It is enough that Frida breathes; this is good.

XI
Dorothy Hale w/Black Dress

An intrinsic feature of

our very own positions of powerlessness, disinheritance
and subordination is wakefulness – fluidity through the
Master-system.

Frida sees what no one else seems to care for: another
body falling at light speed from the top floor of the
Hampshire House building in New York City. It is
Dorothy Hale on the twenty-first of October, nineteen
thirty-eight wearing a black dress, smiling, translucent
like candle wax, bleeding out into the frame of her
suicide. Yet, between the top and bottom of Dorothy
Hale's flight there is a web or better, a finery of spun
hairs and fibers, a new tubing going into the sea, growing
at a higher rate, multiplying without direction, a fission
inside the palm of the air, out from the falling wind
tunnels and there – in this spinning sheaf, in this arc of
eyebrow spirals – a new life unfolds, swells, moistens,
escapes.

XII
Style, Genre & Craft

To call

the making of the body-cast a *style*, is erroneous – this implies loyalty to the Master-sculptor. To say *genre* is false – this implies residence in the Master house, to say *craft* is evil, even though evil does not exist.

Only the Master-writer knows style, genre and craft; the bearing out, bit by bit, (through hard, devoted labor and academy) of the final literary machination that directs, influences, guides and sweeps an entire macro-globe of orientations, moods, fantasy and interests of Master-power.

XIII
The Ecstasy of Occupation

When *He* covers us, we occupy *Him.*

For us – when the virus slips through the capillary,

the cytoplasm's circumference patrols – it is a matter of
ecstasy, and most of all, occupation. Yet, it is an
occupation without installation, without regime. We are
here – momentarily, afloat, gliding, taking half-shapes
into motion.

We are not interested in the full (Master) body. As the
Virus eats away at the Master-figure, a bizarre drama of
features begins to play out its new form in the frame – a
more malleable and vulnerable figure that can be wound
up and made to speak, or better yet, a figure that props
itself up (at a distance) so we can continue our target
practice.

XIV
The Finery of the Virus

To accomplish

the pliability of the target (for this funny drama) it can be said that we use the elasticity of our own voices. It can also be said that it is preferable that we also invite the audience to fill-in the figure's verbiage because the Master-tongue is frayed, porous now – losing its authorities. In essence, there is no voice. A voice box without a will of its own has appeared (the finery of the virus accomplishes this).

XV
Even if in Indigo

A clue:

we are not a Master-projection as the Master would like
you to believe even if in indigo, even if in a possessed,
skinless hue. I will give you a better and positive sign to
work with – we are agile, without definition, without a
cross to carry, with a piece of flame only –

a tiny, ferocious flame shred. When they see us coming,
let them translate. They are so good at translating – this is
because the voices of the Shattered creates a sense of
intimacy, the most provocative and sacred precursor of
enslavement.

XVI
Hat Makers

So many years

the Master has feared our speech. He even assumed he
could install our voices in his den and in this way
cautiously examine and visit on occasion. So, he called on
his architects; so many museums still remain with our
names inscribed, ready for our bones, our coppery bone
fragments. And now he sends his public emissaries. He
sends his dilettantes and hat-makers with streamers; calls
Frida with a delicate hand bell: come here, little one, try
this on, it will be cold soon, come and be warm – come in
time for the next century.

"The next century can be yours," he says.
"It is tattered, yet, it can be yours..."
(He pats her on the back).

XVII
Mater Dolorosa

We watch carefully,

with clown-like eyes askance, we note his muzzle-like
beak opening. We give the Master an old garment, the
one he gave us long ago in the shape of bread and wine,
or in the figure of a Mater Dolorosa, – we did not wear it
(never). And he bends, sips, takes it. Roars.

XVIII
Petite (next to Him)

Death, rape,

incest, mutilation, genocide, forced marriage – at the grip
of the Master: litera-coitus (the Master – penetration).

He casts us in a smaller shape than he; this is why Frida
appears so petite next to Him: in a simulated language
close to his but not true like his; with his wide-hipped
clothes and her hair snipped off, cast on the floor, maybe,
but not in his uncrippled gait, with his lively fragrance,
many times with his name, his orb, even his last name,
maybe, but not his synthesis, his full and solid self, but
not his wall-size Letters.

Why do I call him my Diego?
He never was and will never be mine, he belongs to himself.
—Diary entry, Frida

XIX
The Game of Color

In the Master Palace,

especially in the Master-bedroom, there is a plate of
cosmetics for the raped serf. The regime attached to this
scene is called the Game of Color.

Now, I know it is a game. I repeat, now. Up to this point
there has been no clear proof or better yet, no erudite
concept (a complete concept without the frayed edges of
desperation) that clarifies the intensities of color.

Again: for us, color has always been cast with the notions
of 'darkening'.
On the other hand, for the Master, color has always been
linked to the ideas of 'shining'.

I am not tragically colored.
—Zora Neale Hurston

XX
Unloosened, Free Tendrils

The Master-tailor

gives us *Chaketa(s)* – let us call this, the *darkening jacket(s)* –
so that we may oblige at a later point, if not immediately
– fitting ourselves into his world, his fleshy readings of
the world, to adopt his letters (shields, language, gesture,
religion, skin and).

It is better to burn the garment(s) and throw the voices
back out and sign with our own unloosened, free
tendrils: our *plakas.*

XXI
Exhale

In another room,

perhaps in another mansion – the Master-game includes
half-finished body-casts, less the left arm and without
windows or Stairways, only a chair, of sorts (a sitting and
painting game that includes our new portraiture). We
float through the move, we exhale as we pass, we are
weightless in the Master-rooms.

We wear no *Chaketas.*

XXII
A Flaw in His System

The Master doesn't know

if we ever wore the *Chaketa(s)*, he doesn't know why we
did not accept the offer, such a fine offer (imagine, our
real-body depended on it); he can't figure where we have
located ourselves in his plan – he thinks there may be a
flaw in his system, just maybe.

Of course, he has auxiliary mechanisms for this; yet,
there is a growing fear (let us use the common term, fear,
here) his growing fear – that we are present in a different
form and shape from the one he expects.

Another clue: we are not in his plan. And we are present.

XXIII
A Bronze-Black

Again:

there is no erudite and complete concept that clarifies the relationships between color intensities – in short, it is highly possible to have a 'darkening' white, a 'muddy' white, a 'deep (even exotic, even 'tragically colored') white', a whitish-brown going into a whitish-red. And yet, the Master palette does not allow this game-move. If so, it would be convenient to have a 'brilliant' black, a 'shiny' brown, a bronze-black going into a bluish-gold. See this: Take away the Master-darkening aspects and substances of a 'deep brown' and you have a black sparkle. You have a Frida with serpentine leaves falling out of her marrow.

Take away the *Chaketa* and you will see.

XXIV
Gold Glittering

Frida was born

on September seventeenth, 1926 at the age of eighteen –
when she was found without clothes, bathed in blood,
sprinkled with gold glitter usually used for patron saints
and ballerina costumes, inside a blown-out metal meat
bus cage – her boyfriend, Alejandro, remained intact.

The doctors put her into a body-cast for the rest of her
years (on and off); she responded by putting on clothes
that could never fit her.

XXV
Blood Bottle

It is

not so much a matter of rational resistance, commitment
to a political struggle, a new beret held in the fist.
Remember, we have no footing in the matter – we do not
desire it. It is more an issue of casually reversing the
given jacket and (even politely) putting it between the
levers, in the blood bottle of the Master's favorite signs
and most indulgent servant: language.

XXVI
Like Bare Existence

The term – *sabotage*, for the moment.

It does have something to do with dis-association from
the Master's banquet. It does have something akin to it
like salt, like sand, like bare existence. To say *sabotage* is
closer than to say *resistance*. To say *sabotage* is closer
than to say *historical re-interpretation* or *intelligibility*.
(All are silly and acts of negation and ultimately, suicide;
imagine merely resisting the Master-who-loves-resistance
in his bedroom parlor games to humor his power. Or to
re-interpret his arts – this is like the gallery critic
disagreeing with the exhibit yet, in the papers, giving it
credence for its installation.)

XXVII
The Brain Hums in the Night

Let's repeat:

To say *sabotage* is to encourage an uncatalogued virus to spread into the innumerable circuits of the Master-host body, swimming in the currents, leaping to the central nervous system unpredictably, unraveling things there, then hiding again in the most obvious cytoplasm of a face skin cell (where it will be denied and chalked up to causes of heat rash) – all while the brain hums in the night.

Sabotage is a random fury of our Frida – exposures, unfettered, our writing, our body-*grafos* / cast-aside.

XXVIII
The Barber-Sculptor

Frida sports a hummingbird

necklace today, the hummingbird that was caged for so
long for wearing a personal rainbow on her breast; there
is a Chinese screen going up in flames above Frida's
braided hair and the combed arm of the monkey caresses
her chin, pursing his lips in the fashion of an accountant
who has arrived at the precise figure. The wide angled
ferns await the next torrent of waters, yet, deep inside
their webbed veins there is a passionate rhythm
beginning to fall in tiny lilac flakes – it is all going up,
straight up from the golden arcs of the solitary chair
where Frida, the raging barber-sculptor sits quietly with
a clean pair of scissors staring across the marbled room,
smallish, to the figure of a man, unkempt, proud with his
usual hat hovering over her tilted body, tilted by his
knife and yet, she wears one dancing ballerina shoe.

XXIX
Cover(s)

Instructions:

Go ahead, come on – take what's on the top shelf, it's OK
if you buy it, indulge for a day. Now, take the cover off of
each text, be forceful, let the emotions loosen a bit, tear
things off, make casting-out gestures with the arms, let
the face grimace; now – come on – now. Move around a
little and spray your letters on the little page; take the
volumes back to their original places – if you are caught
just say you are simply *re-turning* them.

XXX
Zero-in

Given the moment –

we zero in on the target, a Master-text before us. Having
paid our own ticket we go up to the booth and aim, the only
thing is that something is going to go awry – we know this,
the bullet has been reshaped. When we pull the trigger, our
insides smile.

XXXI
Pendulum Scissors

Let's put this another way.

The Master-reader's existence depends on the shaping
and production of the *Cover*. This produces many
meanings and effects for everything that follows – the
story, the narrator, the pendulum-scissors in the center of
the book seam, above all. To put it simply – the time has
come to sever the pendulum chain, yet to do this you
may leave the pendulum intact – all that has to be done is
to cross-out the cover with an anti-cover. This is
expedient. Everyone retains their positions in the Master-
system, the only difference is that the system is falling
and contracting now rather than rising and expanding.
We know it can rise again, so we prepare. We cannot
afford to wait for permission and most of all for Reason –
otherwise, the Master-cutter will say to us:

I only gave you a few small nips

(*Unos Cuantos Piquetitos*)

XXXII
Cross-Word

No explanation is necessary.

Everything is reshaped here – a cross-word puzzle is most refreshing. The reader can draw the puzzle in any shape relative to her or his proclivities; the following questions will serve as the motives and forces for the internal moves, i.e., solutions that will create the hidden boundaries of the cross-word.

Across
1. Where was the Master born?
2. What does Master signify?
4. When was this Master released?
5. What language does the Master speak?
6. How long did it take for the Master to arrive at this point?
7. What is the Master's favorite form of art?

Down
1. In what country does Frida find exile?
2. How dark is Frida's jacket?
3. When will Frida find Mexico?
4. How fast does Frida's body-cast multiply?
5. In what precise spot is her exile, her ecstasy?

6. Why is Frida rarely seen laughing?
7. What is her relationship to the Master?
8. If there are two Fridas, who is the third?

XXXIII
The Native

In the Master-landscape

there is an odd figure usually and initially assigned the
role or game-move as 'the Native'.

Here, the logical position or set of game choices is set in a
forum and plenary of naked oppression and
reminiscence; the Master-voice box intervenes and says,
"It stands to reason that the native is reminiscent; he
thinks of the days when he acted out a more powerful
station – a primordial era, his mythologies are a sacred
cluster of these moments."

"Conjure this," the Master says. "Conjure that," he sings,
bristles, retreats and then – *He* reminisces.

XXXIV
The Conceit

For us the conceit lies in the following questions:

1. Who is the Native? Who is Frida?
2. How far back must we go to become the native, how far forward to be?
3. If we are not the Native, is our identity dependent, contingent?
4. If our identity is not contingent, is it necessary?

The conceit lies in a portable and sugary archeology of signs; the collapse of *Memoria(s)* – It is not that we are interested in re-constructing our past to vindicate our present (much in a similar, yet inverse fashion as the Master who diligently scaffolds his logos in order to avoid and deny his past deeds).

We are more intent on another gesture, a dance maybe; an awkward, purposeful, hunched mountain and street urban Frida shuffle, one that resembles something on the other side of the dominant histories yet, something that never existed – that is ours.

XXXV
A Sickle Below

There comes a time

when the *Chaketa* (if it is reversed, cast out, over-taken,
turned upon itself) becomes a *Plaka.*

What happens, for example, when you paint the body
cast, carve a blaze over the sternum area, a sickle below
the right ventricle and then you place it all in an
unexpected exhibit, say, at a mall next to a crocodile
purse or Parisian striped pull-over? The *Plaka* speaks
back in a rash voice, careless, perhaps, even flaunting the
attempted erasure of its designs; it is not concerned with
manners, nor wholeness nor its own systems and
edifications. It is good enough that it throws back and
kicks out to society, to language itself, a forced-upon set
of signs – for a moment, only – for a micro-moment.

XXXVI
Powerlessness & Being

We do not fall

into the inevitable abyss of the Master's game stale-mate:
despair, nausea, hollowness and the one-dimensionality
of human power.

Having no *Chaketa*, putting up the body-cast for exhibit,
implies dispossession, squalor, genocide, (many
injections) – not only in a present sphere of political and
cultural elaborations, but, in a timeless inextricable web
of powerlessness and being. Yet, are such gestures the
key moves in a pernicious Master-scheme?

We reject the game with *Plakas*.

XXXVII
The Mirror in the Canopy

There is something else to remember:
the mirror in the canopy does not exist.

The Master-game lacks ecstasy. Lacks the piano-like steps
that ascend into the soul of the sea anemone, the
tremulous valley where a crystalline alphabet unwinds
its translucent wisdom – a note, a dance, lit with moon
bits of gold. Here is something to keep in mind – the
thousand dreams in a grain of sand. And what is more –
the eerie calling of the sand in our own waking hours at
the office, at the Market Palace where Frida, the bride-to-
be takes a number on a wire and the groom-to-be walks
out with a bundle of arsenic, jams it into his glove
compartment and later ponders on the time-dial
wrapped around his thorax, he ponders – on the absences
kicking out from his thin skin, he works on this, alone,
maybe with the radio on, he considers all this again.

XXXVIII
White Horse with Eight Secrets

The groom

is a bit late for everything as he looks out the window
into the empty street. Comes back to the bathroom and
stares into the mirror and this time, this real (fine) time
there is no mirror. And what does he see? He sees foam,
off-white waves with tiny batwing, rubbery faces inside
of frozen glaciers pushing through the gauze on the wall.
And what does he say, do, wish, ask, cry? The Master-
circus proposes a white horse with eight secrets to be
unraveled throughout the course of his lifetime:
separation, cold weather, resentment, specificity,
velocity, thirst, simulation and hope-shards. The white
horse can appear as a locomotive, a motorcycle – a
televised empire about to rise into prominence – even a
smooth outline of a mustache on the Presidential man.
There is nothing to say, the groom says.

Epilogue
Clay Sheets of Assumption

Only a rush

of image, sharp dust catching the eye for a stanza or two
– at best. All of this is inconsequential, the groom says.
He knows he says it. He drinks a cup of water, relaxes.
Far away, Frida, the bride is not a bride.

She is entirely different.

She is entirely different and walks on another shore.
Maga, she may be called. No one knows.

She does not think in the same manner as the groom; for
her there is no glacier beyond the docks, no tick-tick
behind the sun. There is no sun. Yet she looks up and
sees everything. And the Master-road is non-existent
where she breathes, where she laughs and runs and
composes the pieces of the sky that have lost their spiked
hats. The tiny trumpet mouth filaments play their music
and tell the earth that Frida is free from the Master-
vessels –

the clay sheets where she has been assumed to live.

About the Author

Juan Felipe Herrera, the first Latino Poet Laureate of the United States and son of Mexican immigrants, grew up in the migrant fields of California.

Appointed as the U.S. Poet Laureate in 2015, Juan Felipe Herrera is the son of migrant farm workers, and was educated at UCLA and Stanford University, and received his MFA from the University of Iowa Writers' Workshop. In addition to publishing more than a dozen collections of poetry, Herrera has written short stories, young adult novels, and children's literature.

In 2012, Herrera was named California Poet Laureate. He has won the Hungry Mind Award of Distinction, the Focal Award, two Latino Hall of Fame Poetry Awards, and a PEN West Poetry Award. His honors include the UC Berkeley Regent's Fellowship as well as fellowships from the National Endowment for the Arts, the Bread Loaf Writers' Conference, and the Stanford Chicano Fellows. He has also received several grants from the California Arts Council. He lives in Fresno, California.

Selected titles also available from Manic D Press:

Fiction:

Painting Their Portraits in Winter: stories by Myriam Gurba

Stealing Cherries: flash fiction by Marina Rubin

Madhouse Fog: a novel by Sean Carswell

Hairdresser on Fire: a novel by Daniel LeVesque

98 Wounds: stories by Justin Chin

Po Man's Child: a novel by Marci Blackman

The Rise & Fall of Third Leg: stories and a novella by Jon Longhi

The Hashish Man & Other Stories by Lord Dunsany

Poetry:

Living Quarters: Poems by Adrienne Su

Wet Reckless: Poems by Cassandra Dallett

The Splinter Factory: Poems by Jeffrey McDaniel

Gutted by Justin Chin

Bang Ditto by Amber Tamblyn

15 Ways to Stay Alive by Daphne Gottlieb

Open Letter to Quiet Light by Francesca Lia Block

The Unreasonable Slug: Poems by Matt Cook

Only Dreaming Sky: Poems by Jack Hirschman

Poetry Slam: The Competitive Art of Performance Poetry
    edited by Gary Glazner

Nonfiction:

MDC: Memoir from a Damaged Civilization by Dave Dictor

Women Street Artists of Latin America: Art Without Fear
    by Rachel Cassandra & Lauren Gucik

Women of the Underground: Art by Zora von Burden

Women of the Underground: Music by Zora von Burden

Trans/Love: Radical Sex, Love & Relationships Beyond the Gender Binary, edited by Morty Diamond

Intersex (For Lack of a Better Word) by Thea Hillman

Stencil Nation: Graffiti, Community, and Art by Russell Howze

In Me Own Words: The Autobiography of Bigfoot by Graham Roumieu

The Civil Disobedience Handbook, edited by James Tracy

Good Advice for Young Trendy People of All Ages, edited by Jennifer Blowdryer

Children:

A Rule is to Break: A Child's Guide to Anarchy by John & Jana

Happy Punks 1 2 3: A Counting Book by John & Jana

43 Monsters by Chuck Webster & Arthur Bradford

The Steampunk Coloring & Activity Book by Phoebe Longhi

Fears of Your Life by Michael Bernard Loggins

These and other Manic D titles are available
in print, digital, and audio formats
wherever books are sold and
online with free shipping at
– www.manicdpress.com –